Camille SAINT-SAËNS

INTRODUCTION ET RONDO CAPRICCIOSO

Op. 28

(1863)

Edited by
Richard W. Sargeant, Jr.

Study Score
Partitur

SERENISSIMA MUSIC, INC.

ORCHESTRA

2 Flutes
2 Oboes
2 Clarinets (A)
2 Bassoons

2 Horns (F)*
2 Trumpets (C)*

Timpani

Violin I
Violin II
Viola
Violoncello
Double Bass

*The present score has been updated for the commonkeys of modern instruments
(Clarinets in A or B-flat, Horns in F, Trumpets in C). Berlioz's original score featured
Horns in C, Trumpets in A, Cornets in A.

Duration: ca. 10 minutes

Premiere:
Probably sometime in 1863 with Pablo Sarasate as soloist
The exact date and orchestra are not presently known.
Saint-Saëns composed the work for Sarasate.

ISBN: 978-1-60874-160-1
This score is a newly reserached and engraved edition
prepared by the editor published for the first time.

Printed in the USA
First Printing: April, 2015

INTRODUCTION ET RONDO CAPRICCIOSO
Op. 28

Camille Saint-Saëns
Edited by Richard W. Sargeant, Jr.

41601

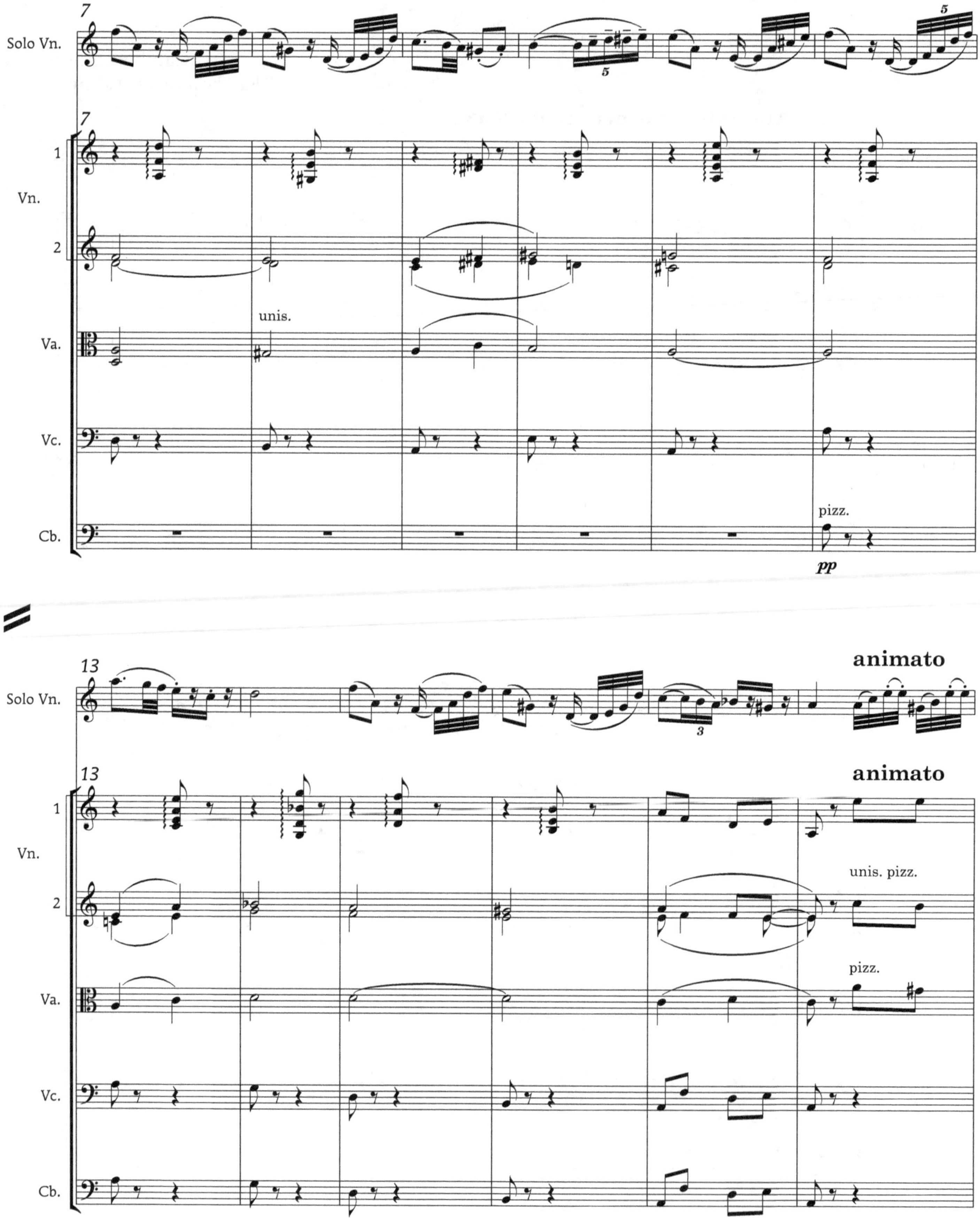

Solo Vn.
Vn.
Va.
Vc.
Cb.
7
unis.
pizz.
pp
animato
animato
13
unis. pizz.
pizz.
5
5
3
5

5
19
Solo Vn.
19
Vn.
1
2
Va.
Vc.
Cb.
arco
pizz.
sf
3
pp
pp
pp
p
p
Tranquillo
23
Solo Vn.
23
Vn.
1
2
Va.
Vc.
Cb.
Tranquillo
arco
sf
p
pp
ppp
arco
p
ppp
arco
p
pp
arco
p
pp
arco
p
pp
41601

27
Solo Vn.
ten.
ten.
27
Vn.
1
div.
2
Va.
Vc.
ppp
Cb.
30
Solo Vn.
marcato
3   3
30
Vn.
1
2
p
Va.
div.
ppp
p
Vc.
ppp
p
Cb.
ppp

37 Allegro ma non troppo ♩. = 88
33
Fl. 1 2
Ob. 1 2
Cl. 1 2
Bn. 1 2
a2
f
Hn. 1 2
Tpt. 1 2
Timp.
Solo Vn.
molto cresc. f f f f
37 Allegro ma non troppo ♩. = 88
33
unis. pizz.
arco
Vn. 1
p
f
dim.
Vn. 2
pizz.
f
dim.
Va.
unis. pizz.
arco
f
dim.
Vc.
pizz.
arco
f
dim.
Cb.
pizz.
arco
p
f
dim.

40
Fl.
Ob.
Cl.
Bn.
Hn.
Tpt.
Timp.
Solo Vn.
40
Vn.
Va.
Vc.
Cb.

46
Fl. 1 2
Ob. 1 2
Cl. 1 2
Bn. 1 2
Hn. 1 2
Tpt. 1 2
Timp.
Solo Vn.
46
Vn. 1
Vn. 2
Va.
Vc.
Cb.
1.
pp
pp
pp
pp
pizz.
arco
pizz.
arco
pizz.
arco
pizz.
arco
pizz.
arco

52
Fl.
Ob.
Cl.
Bn.
Hn.
Tpt.
Timp.
Solo Vn.
Vn.
Va.
Vc.
Cb.
pp
pp
pp
pp
pp
1.
pizz.
arco

58
Fl.
Ob.
Cl.
Bn.
Hn.
Tpt.
Timp.
Solo Vn.
Vn.
Va.
Vc.
Cb.
pp
1.
a2
58

64
Fl. 1 2
Ob. 1 2
1.
Cl. 1 2
Bn. 1 2
a2
Hn. 1 2
Tpt. 1 2
Timp.
Solo Vn.
64
Vn. 1
2
Va.
Vc.
Cb.

72
70
Fl. 1 2
Ob. 1 2
Cl. 1 2
Bn. 1 2
Hn. 1 2
Tpt. 1 2
Timp.
Solo Vn.
pp
tr
tr
70
72
pizz.
arco
Vn. 1
pizz.
arco
2
pizz.
arco
Va.
pizz.
arco
Vc.
pizz.
arco
Cb.

75
Fl. 1 2
Ob. 1 2
1.
pp
Cl. 1 2
pp
Bn. 1 2
1.
pp
Hn. 1 2
Tpt. 1 2
Timp.
Solo Vn.
tr
tr
tr
3
3
3
3
75
Vn. 1
2
Va.
Vc.
pizz.
Cb.
pizz.

80
Fl. 1 2
Ob. 1 2
Cl. 1 2
Bn. 1 2
Hn. 1 2
Tpt. 1 2
Timp.
Solo Vn.
80
Vn. 1
Vn. 2
Va.
Vc.
arco
Cb.
arco

85
Fl.
Ob.
Cl.
Bn.
Hn.
Tpt.
Timp.
Solo Vn.
Vn.
Va.
Vc.
Cb.
pp
pp
pp
p
p
tr
tr
3
3
f
pizz.
pizz.
pizz.
pizz.
pizz.

90
Fl. 1 2
Ob. 1 2
Cl. 1 2
Bn. 1 2
Hn. 1 2
Tpt. 1 2
Timp.
Solo Vn.
90
Vn. 1
2
Va.
Vc.
Cb.
p
p
p
p
p
arco
sfpp
arco
sfpp
arco
pizz.
arco
pizz.
arco
pizz.
fp
f

94
Fl. 1 2
Ob. 1 2
Cl. 1 2
Bn. 1 2
Hn. 1 2
Tpt. 1 2
Timp.
Solo Vn.
94
Vn. 1
Vn. 2
Va.
Vc.
Cb.
p
p
p
pp
sfpp
sfpp
pp
pp
arco
pizz.
arco
arco
pizz.
pizz.
arco

98
Fl. 1 2
Ob. 1 2
Cl. 1 2
1.
pp
Bn. 1 2
1.
pp
Hn. 1 2
Tpt. 1 2
Timp.
Solo Vn.
98
Vn. 1
pizz.
Vn. 2
pizz.
Va.
pizz.
Vc.
Cb.

20
102
105
Fl. 1 2
Ob. 1 2
Cl. 1 2
Bn. 1 2
Hn. 1 2
Tpt. 1 2
Timp.
Solo Vn.
tr tr tr
15
fp
f
f
f
a2
f
f
f
f
105
102
Vn. 1
2
Va.
Vc.
Cb.
arco
arco
arco
arco
arco
f
f
f
f
f
41601

106
Fl. 1 2
Ob. 1 2
Cl. 1 2
Bn. 1 2
Hn. 1 2
Tpt. 1 2
Timp.
Solo Vn.
106
Vn. 1
Vn. 2
Va.
Vc.
Cb.
pp
pp
pp
pp
p
p
p
p
p
pizz.
pizz.
pizz.
pizz.
pizz.

112
Fl.
Ob.
Cl.
Bn.
Hn.
Tpt.
Timp.
Solo Vn.
112
Vn.
Va.
Vc.
Cb.
1.
pp
pp
arco
arco
arco
arco
arco

118
Fl. 1 2
Ob. 1 2
pp
pp
Cl. 1 2
Bn. 1 2
pp
Hn. 1 2
1.
pp
Tpt. 1 2
Timp.
Solo Vn.
cresc.
118
Vn. 1
2
Va.
Vc.
Cb.

123
Fl. 1 2
Ob. 1 2
cresc.
Cl. 1 2
cresc.
Bn. 1 2
p
Hn. 1 2
p
Tpt. 1 2
Timp.
Solo Vn.
f
3 3 3
123
Vn. 1
pizz.
cresc.
Vn. 2
pizz.
cresc.
Va.
pizz.
cresc.
Vc.
pizz.
cresc.
Cb.
pizz.
cresc.

127
126
Fl. 1 2
Ob. 1 2
Cl. 1 2
Bn. 1 2
Hn. 1 2
Tpt. 1 2
Timp.
8va
Solo Vn.
3
127
126
Vn. 1
2
Va.
Vc.
Cb.
arco
arco
arco
arco
arco
f
ff
f
ff
f
ff
f
ff
f
ff
ff
ff
f
ff
f
ff
f
ff
f
ff
f
ten.
ten.
ten.
ten.

130
Fl. 1 2
Ob. 1 2
Cl. 1 2
Bn. 1 2
Hn. 1 2
Tpt. 1 2
Timp.
Solo Vn.
130
Vn. 1
Vn. 2
Va.
Vc.
Cb.
a2
sf
sf
ff

135
Fl. 1 2
Ob. 1 2
Cl. 1 2
Bn. 1 2
Hn. 1 2
Tpt. 1 2
Timp.
Solo Vn.
135
Vn. 1
Vn. 2
Va.
Vc.
Cb.
p
p
p
f

140
Fl. 1 2
Ob. 1 2
Cl. 1 2
Bn. 1 2
Hn. 1 2
Tpt. 1 2
Timp.
sul G
Solo Vn.
3 3
140
Vn. 1
2
Va.
Vc.
Cb.

144
Fl. 1 2
Ob. 1 2
p
Cl. 1 2
p
Bn. 1 2
Hn. 1 2
p
Tpt. 1 2
Timp.
Solo Vn.
144
Vn. 1
2
Va.
Vc.
pizz.
p
Cb.
pizz.
p

148
151
Fl. 1 2
Ob. 1 2
dim.
Cl. 1 2
dim.
Bn. 1 2
Hn. 1 2
dim.
Tpt. 1 2
Timp.
Solo Vn.
dim.
p
148
151
Vn. 1
pp
2
pp
Va.
pp
arco
Vc.
pp
Cb.

152
Solo Vn.
con morbidezza (with tenderness)
152
Vn.
1
2
Va.
Vc.
Cb.
157
Solo Vn.
157
Vn.
1
2
Va.
Vc.
Cb.

162
Fl. 1 2
Ob. 1 2
Cl. 1 2
Bn. 1 2
Hn. 1 2
Tpt. 1 2
Timp.
Solo Vn.
162
Vn. 1
2
Va.
Vc.
Cb.
pizz.
pp

167
Fl.
Ob.
Cl.
Bn.
Hn.
a2
pp
Tpt.
Timp.
Solo Vn.
cresc. poco a poco
167
Vn.
Va.
Vc.
Cb.
pp

34
172
Fl. 1 2
Ob. 1 2
Cl. 1 2
a2
pp
Bn. 1 2
Hn. 1 2
Tpt. 1 2
Timp.
pp
Solo Vn.
172
Vn. 1
2
Va.
Vc.
Cb.
pp

177
Fl. 1 2
Ob. 1 2
Cl. 1 2
Bn. 1 2
1.
pp
Hn. 1 2
Tpt. 1 2
Timp.
Solo Vn.
3
177
div.
1
poco cresc.
Vn.
div.
2
poco cresc.
Va.
poco cresc.
Vc.
poco cresc.
Cb.
poco cresc.

181
Fl. 1 2
Ob. 1 2
Cl. 1 2
Bn. 1 2
Hn. 1 2
Tpt. 1 2
Timp.
Solo Vn.
181
Vn. 1
Vn. 2
Va.
Vc.
Cb.

184
Fl. 1 2
Ob. 1 2
Cl. 1 2
p
Bn. 1 2
Hn. 1 2
Tpt. 1 2
Timp.
Solo Vn.
dim.
1.
p
1.
p
1.
184
unis. pizz.
p
arco
Vn. 1
unis.
p
Va.
p
pizz.
p
arco
Vc.
arco
Cb.
p

188
Fl. 1 2
Ob. 1 2
Cl. 1 2
Bn. 1 2
Hn. 1 2
Tpt. 1 2
Timp.
Solo Vn.
p
188
Vn. 1
pp
2
pp
Va.
Vc.
pp
Cb.

192
Solo Vn.
8va
192
Vn.
1
2
Va.
Vc.
Cb.
196
(8)
Solo Vn.
cresc.
196
Vn.
1
2
Va.
Vc.
Cb.

199
Fl. 1 2
Ob. 1 2
Cl. 1 2
Bn. 1 2
a2
Hn. 1 2
Tpt. 1 2
Timp.
Solo Vn.
13
sf
dim.
199
Vn. 1
2
Va.
Vc.
Cb.
f
pp
p

203
Fl.
Ob.
Cl.
Bn.
Hn.
Tpt.
Timp.
Solo Vn.
Vn.
Va.
Vc.
Cb.
pp
pp
cresc.
p
pizz.
arco

208
Fl.
Ob.
Cl.
Bn.
Hn.
Tpt.
Timp.
Solo Vn.
cresc.
208
Vn.
Va.
Vc.
Cb.
1.
1.

213
Fl. 1 2
Ob. 1 2
Cl. 1 2
Bn. 1 2
Hn. 1 2
1.
pp
Tpt. 1 2
Timp.
pp
ppp
Solo Vn.
p
3
3
cresc.
213
Vn. 1
2
Va.
Vc.
Cb.

217
Fl.
Ob.
Cl.
Bn.
Hn.
Tpt.
Timp.
Solo Vn.
Vn.
Va.
Vc.
Cb.
cresc.
cresc.
p
p
p
f
217
pizz.
cresc.
pizz.
cresc.
pizz.
cresc.
pizz.
cresc.
pizz.
cresc.
3
3
3

220
Fl.
Ob.
Cl.
Bn.
Hn.
Tpt.
Timp.
Solo Vn.
8va
3
Vn.
Va.
Vc.
Cb.
arco
ten.
f
ff

224
Fl. 1 2
Ob. 1 2
Cl. 1 2
Bn. 1 2
Hn. 1 2
Tpt. 1 2
Timp.
Solo Vn.
Vn. 1
Vn. 2
Va.
Vc.
Cb.
a2
sf
ff

229
Fl. 1 2
Ob. 1 2
Cl. 1 2
Bn. 1 2
Hn. 1 2
Tpt. 1 2
Timp.
Solo Vn.
229
Vn. 1
Vn. 2
Va.
Vc.
Cb.
p
pp
p
pp
1.
1.
p
pp
f
p
p

235
Fl. 1 2
Ob. 1 2
Cl. 1 2
pp
Bn. 1 2
Hn. 1 2
pp
Tpt. 1 2
Timp.
Solo Vn.
espress.
sf
235
Vn. 1
pp
2
pp
Va.
p
mf
p
Vc.
p
mf
p
Cb.
pp

241
Fl.
Ob.
Cl.
Bn.
Hn.
Tpt.
Timp.
Solo Vn.
Vn.
Va.
Vc.
Cb.
mf
sf
tr
sf
legg.
241
p
p
pp
p
mf
p
pp
p
mf
pp
p
p

248
Fl. 1 2
Ob. 1 2
Cl. 1 2
dim.
p
dim.
Bn. 1 2
Hn. 1 2
Tpt. 1 2
Timp.
Solo Vn.
dolce
248
Vn. 1
dim.
pp
Vn. 2
dim.
pp
Va.
dim.
pp
Vc.
dim.
pp
Cb.
dim.
pp

255
Fl. 1 2
Ob. 1 2
Cl. 1 2
Bn. 1 2
1.
pp
Hn. 1 2
Tpt. 1 2
Timp.
Solo Vn.
tr
tr
tr
pp
255
Vn. 1
leggierissimo
2
leggierissimo
Va.
leggierissimo
Vc.
Cb.

265
Fl. 1 2
Ob. 1 2
pp
Cl. 1 2
Bn. 1 2
Hn. 1 2
Tpt. 1 2
Timp.
Solo Vn.
tr
tr
tr
tr
3
265
Vn. 1
2
Va.
Vc.
Cb.

270
a2
Fl. 1 2
Ob. 1 2
Cl. 1 2
pp
p
Bn. 1 2
p
Hn. 1 2
p
Tpt. 1 2
Timp.
pp
Solo Vn.
3
f
270
pizz.
Vn. 1
p
2
Va.
pizz.
Vc.
p
pizz.
Cb.
p

274
Fl. 1 2
Ob. 1 2
Cl. 1 2
Bn. 1 2
Hn. 1 2
Tpt. 1 2
Timp.
Solo Vn.
dim.
p
274
Vn. 1
arco
p
2
p
Va.
p
Vc.
arco
p
Cb.
arco
p
1.
p
1.
p
1.

281
278
a2
a2
a2
a2
a2
a2
f
f
f
f
f
Fl. 1 2
Ob. 1 2
Cl. 1 2
Bn. 1 2
Hn. 1 2
Tpt. 1 2
Timp.
Solo Vn.
cresc.
f
281
278
Vn. 1
2
Va.
Vc.
Cb.
f
f
f
f
f

282
Fl.
Ob.
Cl.
Bn.
Hn.
Tpt.
Timp.
Solo Vn.
f
dim.
282
Vn.
Va.
Vc.
Cb.

286
Fl. 1 2
Ob. 1 2
1.
f brillante
Cl. 1 2
Bn. 1 2
Hn. 1 2
Tpt. 1 2
Timp.
Solo Vn.
p
286
pizz.
Vn. 1
p
pizz.
2
p
pizz.
Va.
p
pizz.
Vc.
p
Cb.

290
Fl. 1 2
Ob. 1 2
Cl. 1 2
Bn. 1 2
Hn. 1 2
Tpt. 1 2
Timp.
Solo Vn.
290
Vn. 1
2
Va.
Vc.
Cb.
f brillante
p
f
p
1.
1.

294
Fl.
Ob.
Cl.
Bn.
Hn.
Tpt.
Timp.
Solo Vn.
Vn.
Va.
Vc.
Cb.
f brillante
f brillante
1.
8va
294
1
2
pizz.
p

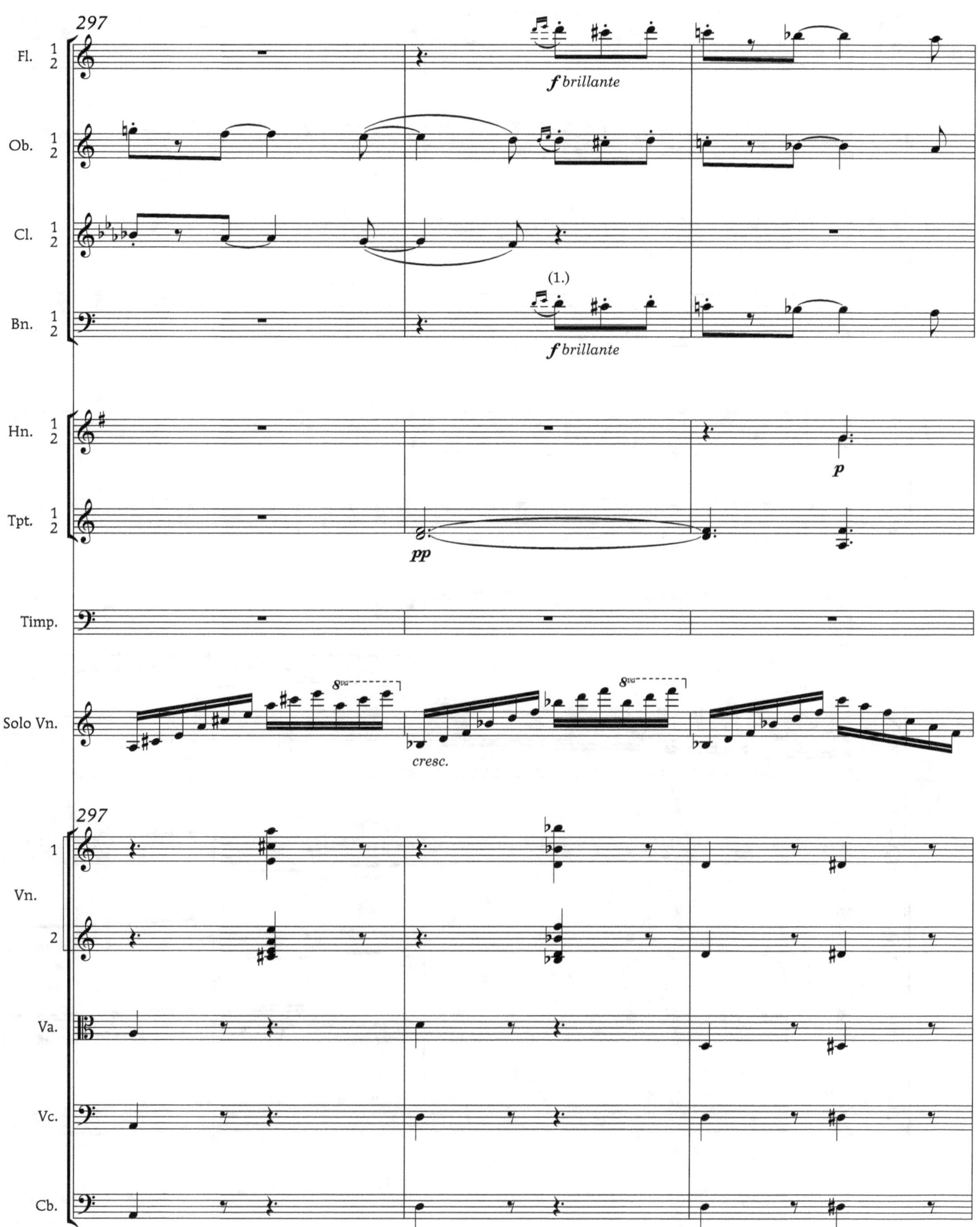
297
Fl.
Ob.
Cl.
Bn.
Hn.
Tpt.
Timp.
Solo Vn.
Vn.
Va.
Vc.
Cb.
f brillante
f brillante
(1.)
p
pp
8va
8va
cresc.
297
1
2

300
Fl. 1 2
Ob. 1 2
Cl. 1 2
Bn. 1 2
Hn. 1 2
Tpt. 1 2
Timp.
Solo Vn.
p
cresc.
p
cresc.
p
cresc.
p
p
pp
tr
f
300
Vn. 1
Vn. 2
Va.
Vc.
Cb.
arco
arco
arco
arco
pizz.
cresc.
pizz.
cresc.
cresc.
pizz.
cresc.
cresc.

ad lib.
a tempo
304
Fl.
Ob.
Cl.
Bn.
Hn.
Tpt.
Timp.
Solo Vn.
ad lib.
a tempo
304
Vn.
Va.
Vc.
Cb.
arco

309 più Allegro ♩. = 120
306
Fl. 1 2
Ob. 1 2
Cl. 1 2
Bn. 1 2
Hn. 1 2
Tpt. 1 2
Timp.
Solo Vn.
dim.
p
dim.
p
dim.
p
dim.
p
dim.
p
p
pp
p
309 più Allegro ♩. = 120
306
Vn. 1
Vn. 2
Va.
Vc.
Cb.
pizz.
pizz.
pizz.
pizz.
pizz.
sf
sf
sf
sf
sf
p
p
p
p
p
arco
arco
arco

311
Fl. 1 2
Ob. 1 2
Cl. 1 2
Bn. 1 2
Hn. 1 2
Tpt. 1 2
Timp.
Solo Vn.
311
Vn. 1
Vn. 2
Va.
Vc.
Cb.
p
p
pp
arco

315
Fl. 1 2
Ob. 1 2
Cl. 1 2
p
Bn. 1 2
Hn. 1 2
Tpt. 1 2
Timp.
pp
Solo Vn.
315
Vn. 1
Vn. 2
Va.
Vc.
arco
Cb.

319
Fl. 1 2
Ob. 1 2
Cl. 1 2
Bn. 1 2
Hn. 1 2
Tpt. 1 2
Timp.
Solo Vn.
319
Vn. 1
Vn. 2
Va.
Vc.
Cb.
fp

323
Fl.
Ob.
Cl.
Bn.
p
Hn.
p
Tpt.
Timp.
Solo Vn.
cresc.
f
323
pizz.
Vn.
pizz.
Va.
pizz.
Vc.
pizz.
Cb.

327
Fl.
Ob.
Cl.
Bn.
Hn.
Tpt.
a2
pp
Timp.
p
Solo Vn.
327
Vn.
f
f
Va.
f
Vc.
f
Cb.
f

331
Fl.
Ob.
Cl.
Bn.
Hn.
Tpt.
Timp.
Solo Vn.
Vn.
Va.
Vc.
Cb.
p cresc.
pp
cresc.
1.
1.
p cresc.
fp subito
molto cresc.
arco
arco
arco
arco
arco
pp
pp
pp
pp
cresc.
cresc.
cresc.
cresc.
cresc.
331

339
Fl.
Ob.
Cl.
Bn.
Hn.
Tpt.
Timp.
Solo Vn.
Vn.
Va.
Vc.
Cb.
a2
a2
a2
a2
f
ff
f
ff
f
ff
f
ff
f
ff
p molto cresc.
f
ff
f
ff
8va
339
f
ff
f
ff
f
ff
ff
f
ff